Our Community and Others

James E. Davis
Educational Consultant
Boulder, Colorado

Contents

Communities in Photographs

These sets of photographs show two ways of looking at a community. The picture on the left in each set was taken from an airplane. This is an aerial photograph. The picture on the right was taken on the ground. It is a ground photograph.

What things can you see in the aerial photograph in each set? What can you see in the ground photograph? Which photograph shows a larger area? Which photograph shows more small things, like windows and bushes?

a

b

Communities in Photographs

Map makers use both kinds of photographs to help them make maps.

From Pictures to Maps

The photograph below shows a place where people work. It is an aerial photograph. What things can you see in this photograph?

The top picture on page 5 is a drawing. The artist made this drawing by looking at the photograph below. What things are in the photograph but not in the drawing?

The picture at the bottom of page 5 is a map of the same area. The map uses symbols. The symbols stand for real things that are in the photograph and the drawing. A map has a legend. A legend is a list of the map's symbols and their meanings.

Photograph

From Pictures to Maps

Drawing

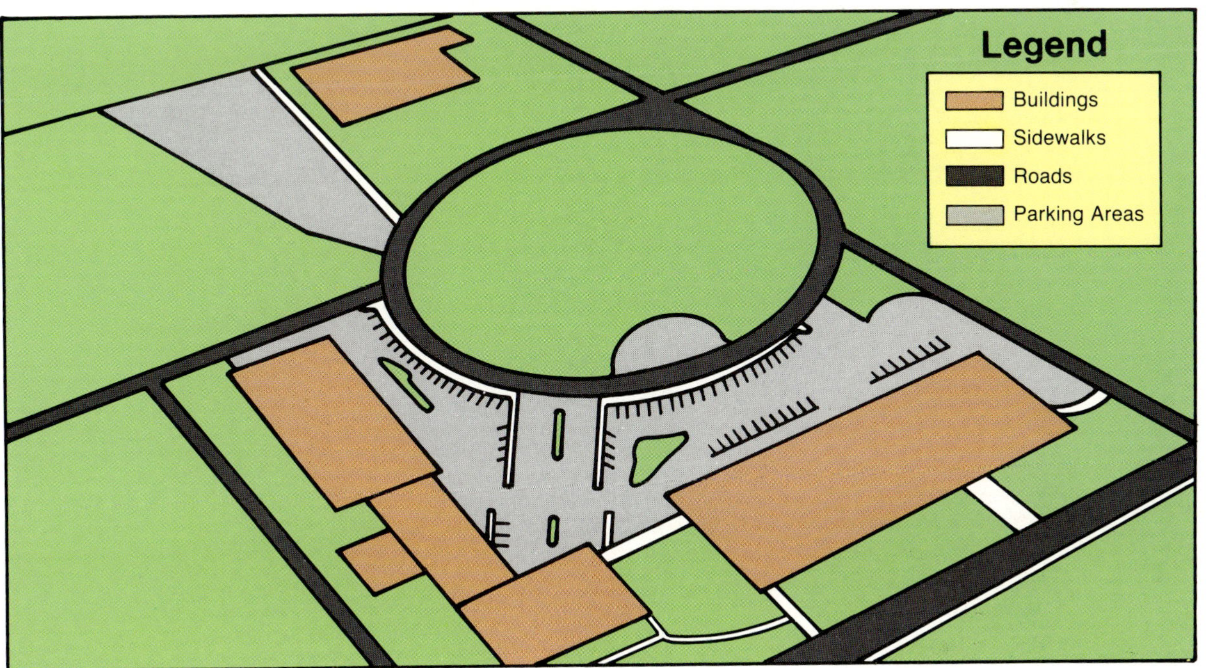

Map

The World of Nature

These are pictures of some natural features. Are any natural features like these near your community?

a. plain

b. stream

c. coast

d. mountain

e. desert

f. lake

The World of People

These pictures show things that people add to the land. When people build these things, they change the land.

a

b

c

d

e

f

Circles and Bars Make Graphs

Counting

Every day, people count things. Think of all the things you might count. How many people are in your family? How many teachers are in your school?

Suppose you want to make a cake. You will need four eggs for this cake. You might count the eggs in your refrigerator to be sure you have enough. Your friend might offer to trade a Frisbee for 20 marbles. How would you know if you have 20 marbles?

Sometimes, a city traffic department counts cars. They count the cars that go past a certain corner. Then, they decide if the corner should have a traffic light.

Tallying

One way to count things is to tally them. To do this, we make tally marks (/) on a chart.

Mr. Conklin is the teacher in one third grade class. He wanted to know which students raised their hands the most. One day, he counted the number of times each student raised his or her hand to answer a question. This chart shows the results for four of his students.

**Number of Times
Students Raised Their Hands**

Name of Student	Tally Marks	Number of Tally Marks
Ann	//	2
Marilee	///// ///	8
Eric	//	2
Ricardo	////	4
Total		16

Circles and Bars Make Graphs

Circle Graph

We can make a picture of the information in the tally chart. We can make a picture called a circle graph. A circle graph shows all the parts that make a total number. Some parts are big. Some parts are small. Look at the parts in this circle graph.

**Number of Times
Students Raised Their Hands**

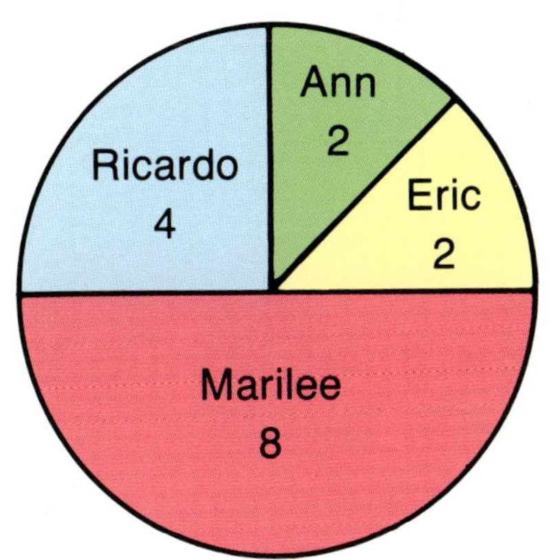

The whole circle stands for the total number of times these students raised their hands. Each part stands for the number of times one student raised his or her hand.

Add the numbers in the parts. Is the total the same as the total on the tally chart? Do you like this way of showing information?

Bar Graph

We can show the same information with another kind of graph. This graph is called a bar graph.

**Number of Times
Students Raised Their Hands**

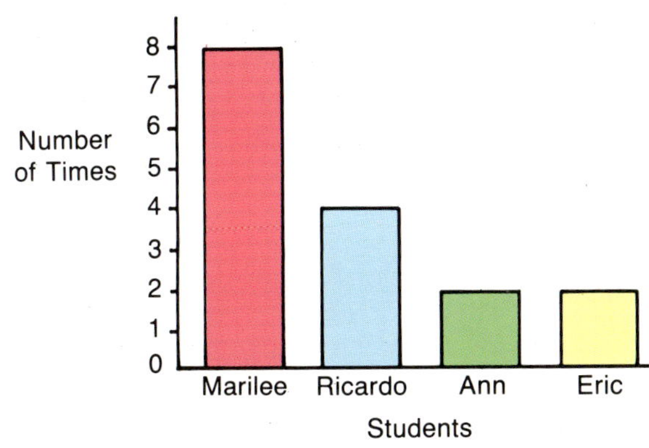

The left side of the bar graph has numbers. The bottom of the graph has names. Above each name is a bar. Each bar goes up to the number of times that student raised her or his hand.

Who raised her or his hand the most?

What is the total number of times all these students raised their hands?

How Far?

One of the cars in these photographs is a real car. The other one is a toy car. Which picture shows the real car? How can you tell?

The car on the right is a scale model of the real car on the left. A scale model is exactly like the real thing. But it is much smaller.

Scale is a small measurement that stands for a larger measurement. A toy car may be 2 inches long. The toy is a scale model of a real car. The real car may be 120 inches long.

A scale model shows what a real thing looks like. If we have a scale model, we do not have to see the real thing.

How Far?

This is a drawing of a finger that is 2 inches long. Does this look like your finger? It may be close to the size of your first finger. In this drawing, the finger is the same size as a real finger.

In this drawing, the same finger is only 1 inch long. This is a scale drawing of the finger. The scale of this drawing is one half, or ½, or 1 to 2. This finger would have to be two times as big to match the first drawing.

In this drawing, the same finger is only ½ inch long. The scale of this drawing is one fourth, or ¼, or 1 to 4. This finger would have to be four times as big to match the first drawing. It would have to be two times as big to match the second drawing.

Maps use scale to show large areas in small spaces. On a map, a small dot may stand for a large city. A short line may stand for a long highway. The scale of a map tells us how big a place really is. It tells us how far one place is from another place. Map scale helps us understand a map.

a. Red Rocks

b. Pearl Street Mall

c. Hospital

d. Justice Center

e. Golf Course

f. Bear Creek School

A City in Symbols

g. Fire Station

h. City Hall

i. Boulder High School

j. City Park

k. Crossroads Mall

l. Scott Carpenter Park

A Place to Live

People build many different kinds of places to live. They build small houses, big houses, and apartment buildings. Some homes were built long ago. Others are quite new.

When people build places to live, they use different kinds of materials. Some homes are made of brick, stone, wood, or even metal.

Why do you think some people build brick houses while others build wooden houses? Why do some people live in small houses with big yards while others live in large apartment buildings?

What is your home like? What is it made of? Does one of these buildings look like your home?

a

b

c

d

A Place to Live

e

f

g

h

i

j

A Place to Work

Men and women work at different jobs. Some people work outside. Some work inside. Some workers build stores and offices. Others work in stores and offices.

Some workers make things for other people. Some do things for other people.

What do the workers in your family do? What kind of work would you like to do?

These pictures show some of the kinds of work people do. Have you seen workers doing these things?

a

b

c

d

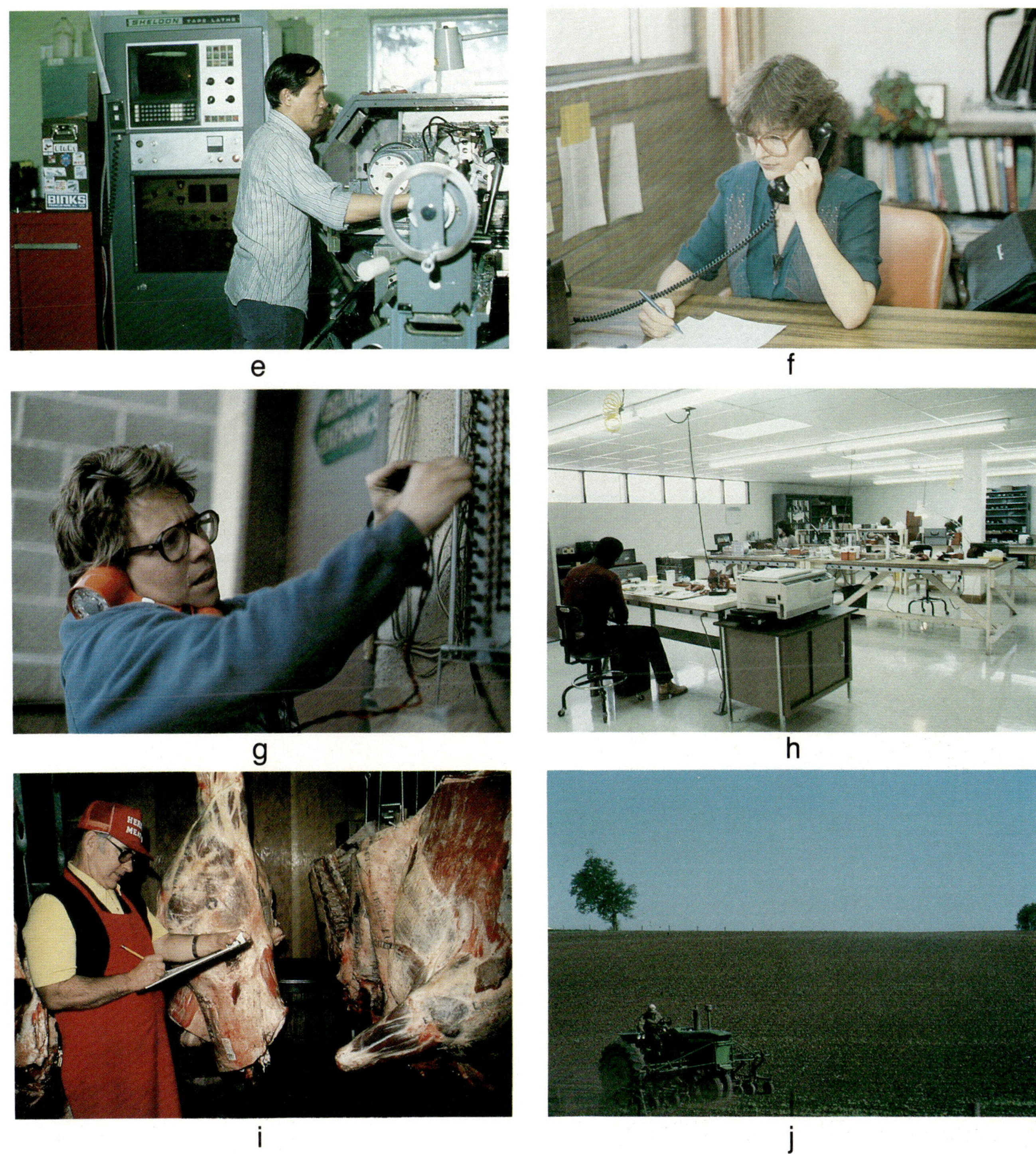

e

f

g

h

i

j

Workers Use Tools

Workers use tools to do their work. Some workers use many tools. Others do not. Some tools are small. Some are very large.

It is easy to learn how to use some tools, like pencils or can openers. It is very difficult to learn how to use other tools. Some workers learn to use big machines, like scoop shovels. Some learn to use microscopes. Some microscopes are small enough to sit on a table. Others are so big they fill a whole room.

What tools do you use when you do school work? What tools does your teacher use?

a

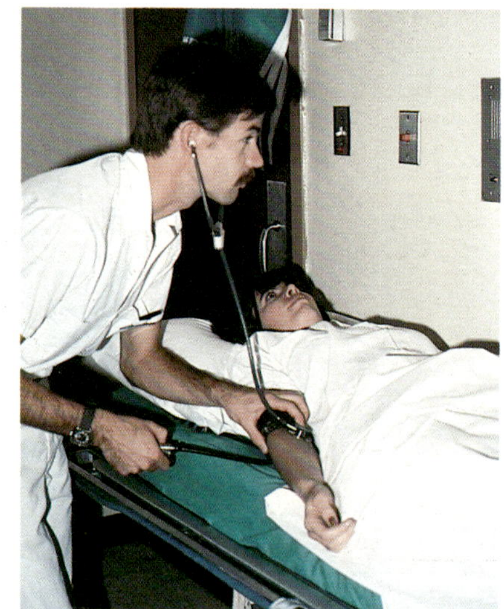

b

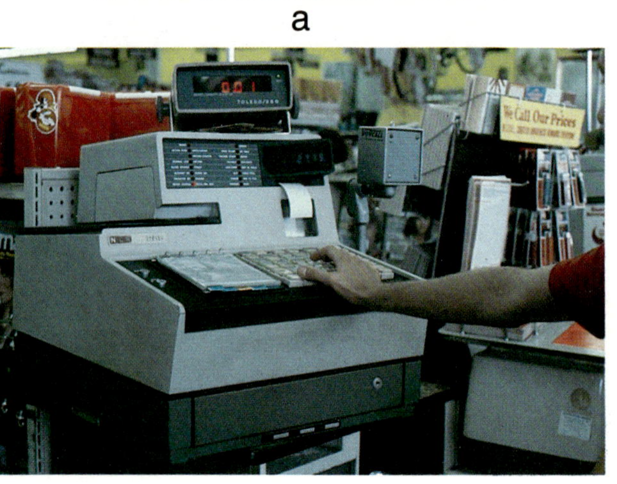

c

d

Workers Use Tools

e

f

g

h

i

j

A Place to Have Fun

Let us look at how people have fun. Sometimes, people like to have fun outdoors. They swim, hike, play ball games, or ski. Sometimes, people have fun indoors. They go to movies or visit museums. They may swim or play ball games indoors.

Sometimes, people like noisy fun. They get together with many friends. They laugh and shout at each other. Sometimes, people want to be quiet. They may read a book alone or play checkers with a friend.

Having fun is important. Having fun makes people happy.

a

b

A Place to Have Fun

c

d

e

f

g

h

4321 Oak Drive
Dallas, Texas 75204
December 1, 1983

Dear Kimberly,
    I got your letter. Thanks. I like the Australian stamps.
    You asked what I do. Well, today I got up. Then I took a shower. I wore my best sweater to school.
    School was O.K. We did mostly reading and math. Then we studied maps. I met a new girl at school. She was nice. We ate lunch together.
    Well, I have to clean up my room.

                Your friend,
                Alice

Making Decisions

Every day we make lots of decisions.

We decide

- what to wear.
- what to eat.
- how to act.
- how to help.
- what to do.

How many decisions do you make in a day?

What happens if you decide not to

- get up in the morning?
- take a bath or a shower?
- brush your teeth?
- go to school?

What happens when you decide to

- make a new friend?
- study hard at school?
- trade for something?
- help around the house?

If I Were a Map

If I were a map
I could show you the way.
I could show you the school
And fine places to play.

I would show places smaller
Than they really are,
But only to bring closer
Things that are far.

I would have many colors—
Blue rivers, green land.
I would even have symbols
to give you a hand.

Cities, towns, buildings, streets—
I would show you all of these—
Lakes and parks and
    swimming pools,
So you could go where you
    please.

Maps are very useful. A map shows places that are close to your home. It shows places that are far away. Maps tell how far one place is from another. They tell how big cities are. A map might show how to get to an airport or to a state park. Another map could show how to get to another country or to an ocean.

Many people need maps. Someone who studies railroads in your state needs a railroad map. A railroad map shows where the railroad tracks go. It also shows the cities the trains go through.

You and your family might need a road map. You would need a road map if you took a trip in your car.

If I Were a Map

Different maps show different kinds of information. Some maps show large areas such as countries. These maps usually do not show all the information about a country. For example, they do not show all cities and towns. There is not enough space on the map to show everything.

Other maps show small areas. A map might show a city, or a neighborhood, or just one block in a neighborhood. Small area maps usually show many details. A map of one city block might show every house or store on that block.

The map below gives basic information about one state. It gives the name of the state. What is the state's name? It shows the boundary of the state. What symbol is used to show the boundary? The map also shows the capital city of the state. What is the name of the capital city? Most maps of Kansas show its name, boundary, and capital city.

The map below also shows three cities in the state besides the capital city. What are the names of the three other cities? The map shows one road in the state. What is the number of that highway? Other maps of Kansas would probably show more cities. They would probably also show more roads.

When you look at different maps, always check to see what information they show.

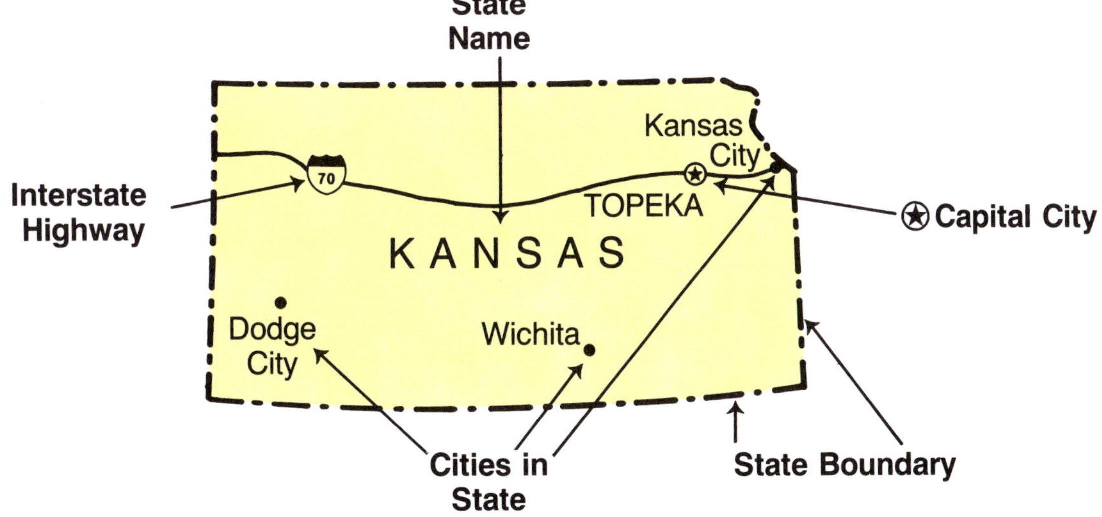

Boulder and Other Communities

In many cities in our country you can buy a McDonald's hamburger. You also can buy Texaco gasoline in many places. You and a friend who lives in another state could shop at department stores that have the same name. What department stores are in many cities? What other businesses have stores in many places in our country?

A company that is in many cities is called a chain business or store. Usually all of its buildings look alike. All businesses in the chain sell or do the same things.

Some stores and businesses are only in one city. The people who own them usually live in the same city. They often work in their stores and businesses. Some of these stores are small. Some are big. They sell hamburgers, clothing, tools, and many other things.

Do you know someone who owns a store in your city? What stores or businesses are only in your city? They are local stores or businesses. They are only in one place.

These are pictures of businesses in Boulder. Which ones do you think might be in your town also? Which ones probably are only in Boulder?

a

b

c

d

e

Does your community have any of the chain businesses pictured here? What other chain businesses can you think of?

Cities are alike and different in other ways. All cities have streets or roads. Some, but not all, cities have a big lake, or a river, or a mountain. What does your city have that most other cities have? What does your city have that only a few other cities have?

Signs of Our Times

a

b

c

d

e

f

g

Boulder Beginnings

What Is History?

One way to learn about a place is to study its history. History is a story about the past.

Think of one thing you did last year. Try to remember something that happened to you in kindergarten or first grade. These things are part of your own history, your own story.

A town or city also has a history. You are going to learn about some of the history of a small city. That city is Boulder, Colorado.

Why Boulder Began

Over a hundred years ago, some people decided to look for gold in Colorado. In the western half of Colorado, there are many mountains. The eastern half is very flat. Streams run down out of the mountains through canyons. Canyons are low places between high mountains. The people who looked for gold followed the streams up the canyons. Some found gold in the streams. Some found gold in the stream and in the mountains near where Boulder is now. One place where they found gold was called Gold Hill. Another place was called Gold Run.

What do you think happened when the gold was found?

Boulder Beginnings

A New Town

In 1859, some of the miners started the town of Boulder. A boulder is a very large rock. There were many large rocks near the stream, or creek, so the miners named their town Boulder. They called the stream Boulder Creek.

Most people believe the first houses in Boulder were built near the red rocks. One record of Boulder's history says the town began at the forked dead tree on the right bank of the creek, just below the red rocks. The red rocks are still there. The forked dead tree is gone, probably rotted away.

At first, Boulder was only two miles long. People built houses and stores on both sides of the creek. The first buildings were near the red rocks. More buildings were built along the creek to the east. Many of the first houses were built along Pearl Street.

Government in Boulder

By 1871, Boulder was a busy, growing town. The square where the courthouse is now had a fence all around it. People from places near Boulder came to the square to sell grain, hay, fence posts, and lumber. They tied their oxen, horses, and mules to the fence around the square.

Boulder's main street was a very busy place. All the animals and the people selling things in the streets made problems. Boulder's newspaper carried stories about the problems in the town. Here are some of the headlines:

Too Many Runaway Animals in Boulder

Pass Laws to Keep Horses Tied Up

Hire a Town Herder to Gather Up the Cows

Children in Places They Should Not Be. Pass New Laws.

Government in Boulder

Because of such problems, the people of Boulder decided to form a city government. The city government made laws to make the town a better place in which to live. What laws do you think the first city government of Boulder made?

Today, Boulder still has a city government. The government offices are now in this building. Many people work for the government to keep Boulder a nice place in which to live.

Living in Early Boulder

The first houses in Boulder were made of logs. The houses were very small. The people who lived in them were called settlers. The settlers cut down big trees and cut them into logs. They cut two flat sides on the logs so they could put one log on top of another. The cold wind blew in through the cracks between these logs. The settlers filled the cracks with clay. The floor of a cabin was the ground.

These early cabins were square. Each side was about six feet long. They usually had only one room. Many cabins had no windows. Can you imagine your family living in such a cabin?

The men and boys who lived in these cabins wore shirts and pants made of cotton or wool. They often wore hats with wide brims. The women and girls wore long skirts and blouses. They had boots or high-topped shoes. In warm weather, the children would go barefoot.

Living in Early Boulder

Traveling in early Boulder was not easy. The roads were just dirt trails. Most people traveled in wagons or buggies pulled by horses or mules. Oxen pulled the biggest wagons. It took a long time to get to another town traveling in wagons on dirt roads.

Some of the children had to travel a long way to school. Some boys and girls lived several miles from Boulder. These children rode horses to the school in town. They tied their horses to trees along Boulder Creek, using long ropes. The horses could wander around eating the grass along the creek while the children were in school. After school, the students rode home to help with the work.

Wild animals lived in the hills west of Boulder. People killed some of them for food. They ate meat from deer, rabbits, squirrels, and even bears. They also picked wild berries. Some of the people planted gardens. The town did not have grocery stores at first, and no one had a refrigerator. They had to eat the food right away because they had no way to store it.

A Little Bit of History

Native Americans and the Settlers

When the first white settlers came to Boulder, they found Native Americans camped close to the Red Rocks. These Native Americans were called the Arapahoe. Their leader's name was Chief Left Hand. Chief Left Hand was afraid the settlers would kill all the animals, burn the woods, and destroy the grass. He told the settlers to go away.

The settlers were worried that there would be many fights with the Arapahoe. But they gave the Arapahoe food and friendship. The Arapahoe made and kept a promise not to fight the settlers.

Some of the Arapahoe lived near Boulder for a few more years. Others moved to valleys that were farther away from Boulder.

The First School

The first school in Boulder was built on what is now called Walnut Street. It was about where Broadway and Walnut Street cross today. This was the first school in the state of Colorado.

The school's first teacher was Abner Brown. Abner Brown helped to build the school house. He made the stove that heated the school in the winter.

The school term was three months long in those days. Abner Brown was paid $1.50 per month for each student. The students' parents paid Mr. Brown. There were 40 students in the first class. They were from six years old to 15 years old.

Once during a school day, seven Arapahoe came into the classroom. The Arapahoe were interested in the drinking cup hanging from the water bucket. They drank water from the cup, and poured water in and out of the bucket with the cup. Then they left.

The children were surprised to have Native Americans as visitors to their school. The Arapahoe probably were surprised to see the children all kept in a schoolroom. Native American children did not go to school. They learned from their parents and from nature.

A Little Bit of History

Railroads in Boulder

The town of Boulder grew because there were many mines in the mountains to the west. Miners came to Boulder to sell their gold and silver. They bought supplies in Boulder to take back to the mountains.

As the town grew, the people decided they needed a railroad. The railroad would bring mining supplies to Boulder's stores. It would carry the miners' gold and silver to other places. The first two railroads in Boulder were the Colorado Central and the Denver-Boulder Valley. These railroads came from Denver to the center of Boulder.

In 1882, the Union Pacific Railroad decided to build a railroad up Boulder Canyon. It took a year to build the railroad. Then in 1894, many of the mines began to close. The gold and silver was running out. In that year there was also a great flood. It rained for six days in the mountains above Boulder. The mountain snow melted. Flood water roared down Boulder Creek and washed out the railroad.

Today, there are two railroads into Boulder. They are the Union Pacific and the Colorado and Southern Railroads. No railroad goes up Boulder Canyon.

An Exploding Pocket

Edward was 12 years old. He lived in Boulder when it was just beginning. One morning, Edward went hunting near his home. He shot two squirrels that his mother could cook for supper.

Edward then decided to go to town and see his friends. He had a mule to ride to town, but he did not have a saddle for the mule. Edward climbed onto the mule's bare, bony back, and they set off for Boulder. Although Edward was not in a hurry, the mule was. It began to trot very fast. Edward bounced up and down on its back.

There was something in his back pocket that Edward had forgotten about. While he was hunting, he had put some gunpowder and a wooden match in his pocket. The mule trotted faster. Edward bounced harder.

Suddenly, the match was hit hard enough to catch fire. It made the gunpowder explode! Edward went sailing through the air! He landed hard on his back. The frightened mule raced to Boulder without Edward.

Edward was lucky. He was not hurt badly. But he never again carried gunpowder and matches in the same pocket.

Carriages and Cars

In 1911, most people in Boulder still rode in carriages and wagons pulled by horses. One man who lived near Boulder had a shiny red car. He was very proud of it.

One morning, the man was driving his car to Boulder. He saw a horse and carriage coming toward him. He stopped and shut off the car's motor. He didn't want to frighten the horse. The carriage stopped, too. The driver started his car again and drove slowly past the carriage.

Just then, the horse reared back and jumped on the front of the car! The horse kicked at the car. Both drivers pulled at the harness to get the horse off the car. When the horse calmed down, the carriage went on its way. The pretty red car was left mashed and dented.

It took a while for the horses in Boulder to get used to the shiny, noisy cars. But in a few years, carriages and cars were seen on Boulder's streets together.

Stories About Boulder

Boulder has changed very much since the old mining days. But one man remembers what it was like then. Eldora is a tiny town in the mountains west of Boulder. At one time, Eldora was a busy mining town.

Binx Rugg still lives in Eldora. Binx, his father, and his grandfather worked in many places in Colorado's Rocky Mountains. In 1897, his father had 20 teams of horses and wagons. He filled the wagons with wood and sold it in the towns near the mountains. His grandfather was the town marshal in Eldora for 30 years. The three men also mined for gold. For a while, they made a lot of money. Binx still owns several mines around Eldora. He has even bought the school building in which he went to school.

Binx liked Boulder when it was just a small town. He helped his father take wagons full of wood to Boulder. He had friends there. Now, Binx thinks Boulder is too big, and he doesn't like to go there. For Binx Rugg, the old towns and the old ways were the best.

Boulder's Main Street

Pearl Street was the first street in Boulder. It started near the Red Rocks and grew eastward, following Boulder Creek. These pictures show how Pearl Street has changed over the years. The dirt and mud were replaced by pavement. Carriages and wagons were replaced by cars. More buildings were built. Street lights were added. And parking meters were placed along the street.

A few years ago, part of Pearl Street was closed off to cars. Buildings were painted and rebuilt. This part of the street has become a shopping mall. There are sidewalks, benches, statues, and flowers where the pavement used to be.

a. This is Pearl Street about 50 years after Boulder became a town.

Boulder's Main Street

b.   This is Pearl Street about ten years ago.

c.   This is the Pearl Street Mall today.

A City Is . . .

A city is people
Who work every day,
Who buy goods and services,
And go out to play.

A city is buildings
Big, tall, and wide
That rise in the streets.
What nice places to hide!

A city is buses
And cars, cabs, and trains
That rush all around
In all sorts of lanes.

A city is fun
With movies and shows
And museums and parks
And what else, who knows?

A city is you.
A city is me.
Come to a city.
It's a great place to see.

Cities, States, and Capitals

a

b

c

d

e

f

Cities, States, and Capitals

Maps tell us about the people who live on the land. One important thing maps tell us is how people divide the land into areas. Land is divided into cities, states, and countries. These areas are called political features. A map that shows political features is a political map. This is a political map of the United States.

Political features are shown on a map with symbols. One kind of symbol is used to show the political area called a state. The United States has 50 states. A symbol shows the boundary of each state. Another symbol shows the capital city of each state.

Cities, States, and Capitals

Maps tell us about the land on earth. Physical maps show features, or parts, of the land. Some physical features are mountains, valleys, rivers, and forests. Physical features are real things that can be seen. They are part of nature. Physical features are natural features.

Physical features are shown on maps with symbols. This is a physical map of the United States. Find the symbols for physical features on this physical map. How does this map tell you where there are hills and mountains? How does it tell you where there are rivers and lakes?

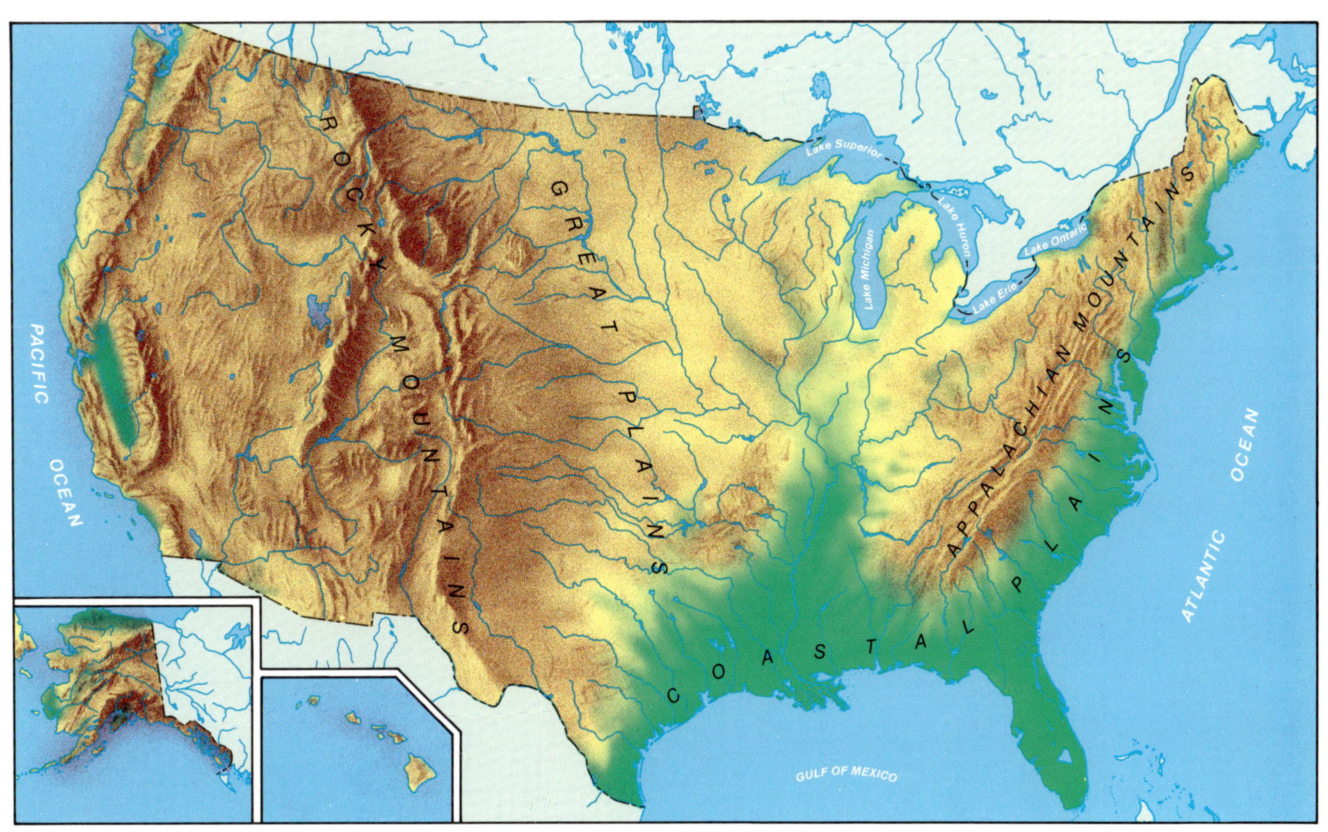

Where On Earth?

The earth is a very large sphere. A sphere is round like a ball. This picture shows the round earth. Astronauts took the picture from their space ship.

Near the center of the picture is the continent of Africa. At the top is a small part of Asia. Part of Antarctica is at the bottom. The Atlantic Ocean is on the left. The Indian Ocean is on the right.

Find these places on a globe.

Where On Earth?

This is a map of part of the earth. It is a map of the area in the photograph on page 48. This map shows that the earth is a sphere.

What continents are on this map? What oceans are on the map? Are these places a long way from the United States of America?

The pictures taken by astronauts have helped map makers draw better maps of the world. Why do you think this is so? What kinds of things do you think map makers study in the pictures taken from space ships?

Cities in Hemispheres

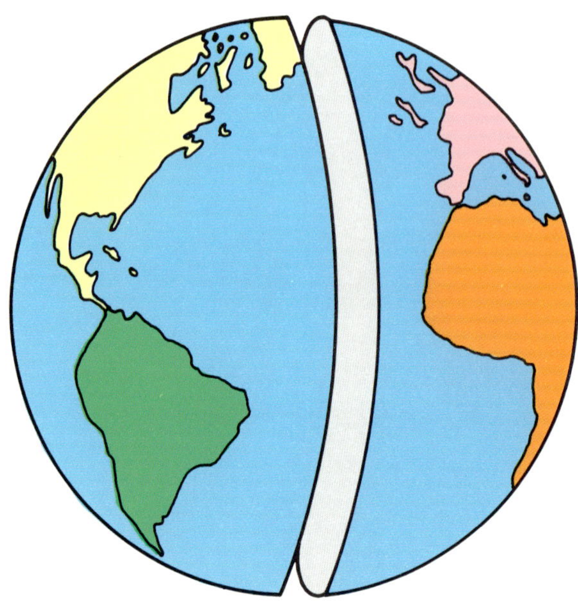

Maps and globes help us understand our world better. Sometimes map makers use imaginary lines on globes and maps. These lines make it easier to see small parts of the world.

One imaginary line used by map makers goes through the North Pole and the South Pole. This line goes north and south around the middle of the earth. It divides the earth into two parts. Each half is called a hemisphere. Hemisphere means half of a sphere or ball.

This picture shows how the earth would look if it came apart at this imaginary line. The part on the left is the Western Hemisphere. The part on the right is the Eastern Hemisphere.

Can you see all of each hemisphere in this picture?

Cities in Hemispheres

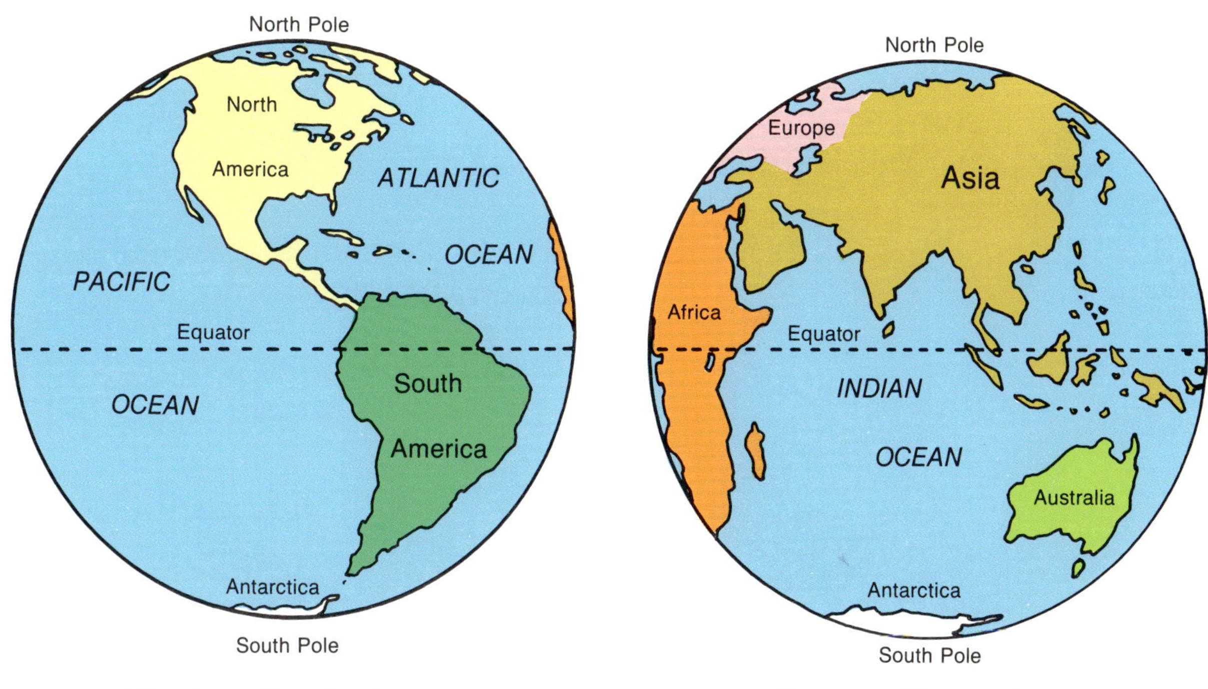

Western Hemisphere　　　　**Eastern Hemisphere**

Pretend you are an astronaut. Your space ship is flying directly above the middle of the Western Hemisphere. The shapes of the earth and the continents look like what you see in the picture on the left.

Do you see some large bodies of land? These are called continents. Do you see two continents that are connected by a thin area of land? These continents are North America and South America. What two oceans are around these continents?

Find the North Pole and the South Pole. Halfway between the North Pole and the South Pole is another imaginary line. It goes the other way around the earth. It goes east and west. This line is called the equator. Find the equator in these pictures.

Your space ship has traveled halfway around the earth. You are now directly above the middle of the Eastern Hemisphere. What you see looks like the picture on the right. What imaginary line is just below you? What continents do you see? What oceans do you see?

Cities in Hemispheres

Map makers use another imaginary line to divide the world into two other parts. This line is called the equator.

The equator goes east and west around the middle of the earth. If the earth could come apart at the equator, it would look like this.

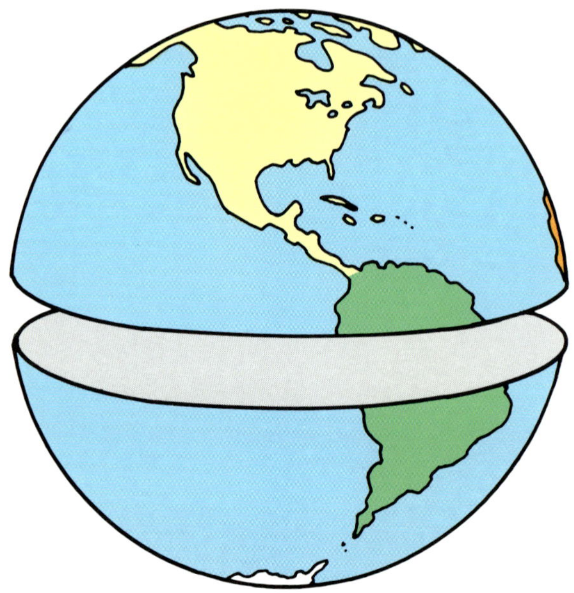

The equator divides the land on earth into two hemispheres. The top half is the Northern Hemisphere. The bottom half is the Southern Hemisphere. The North Pole is the center of the Northern Hemisphere. The South Pole is the center of the Southern Hemisphere.

Cities in Hemispheres

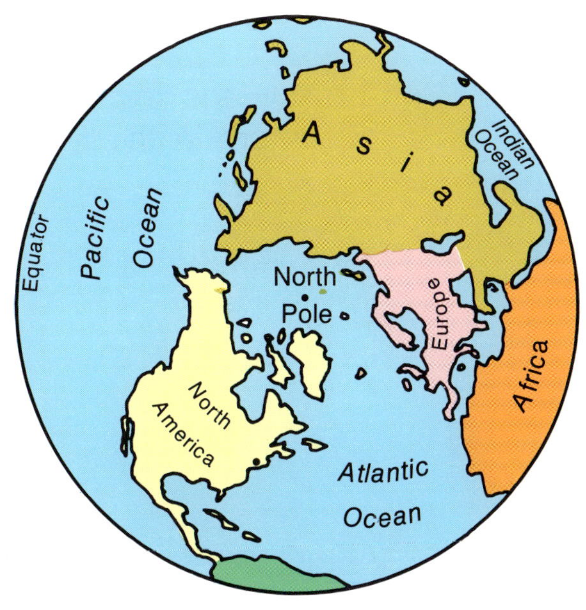

Northern Hemisphere

You are in your space ship directly above the North Pole. This is what you see. You are looking at the Northern Hemisphere.

Is the North Pole on land or on water? What continents and oceans can you see? Where is the equator?

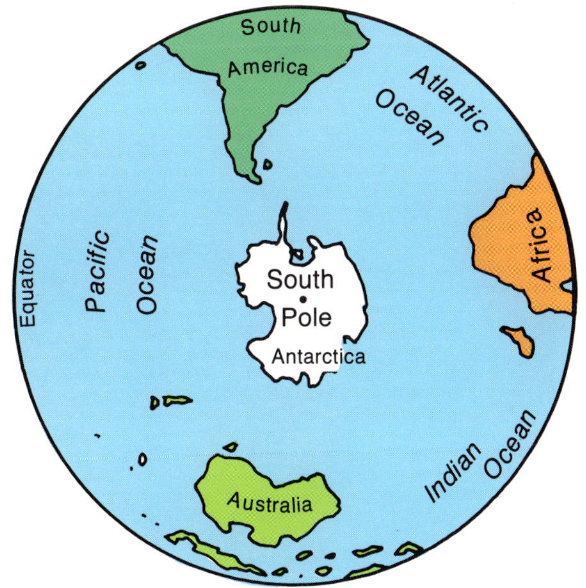

Southern Hemisphere

Now you are above the South Pole. Is the South Pole on land or on water?

What new continents can you see? What other continents can you see? How many oceans are in the Southern Hemisphere?

Cities in Other Countries

This map shows the whole earth flattened out. Flat maps of the earth are hard to make. Why do you think this is so?

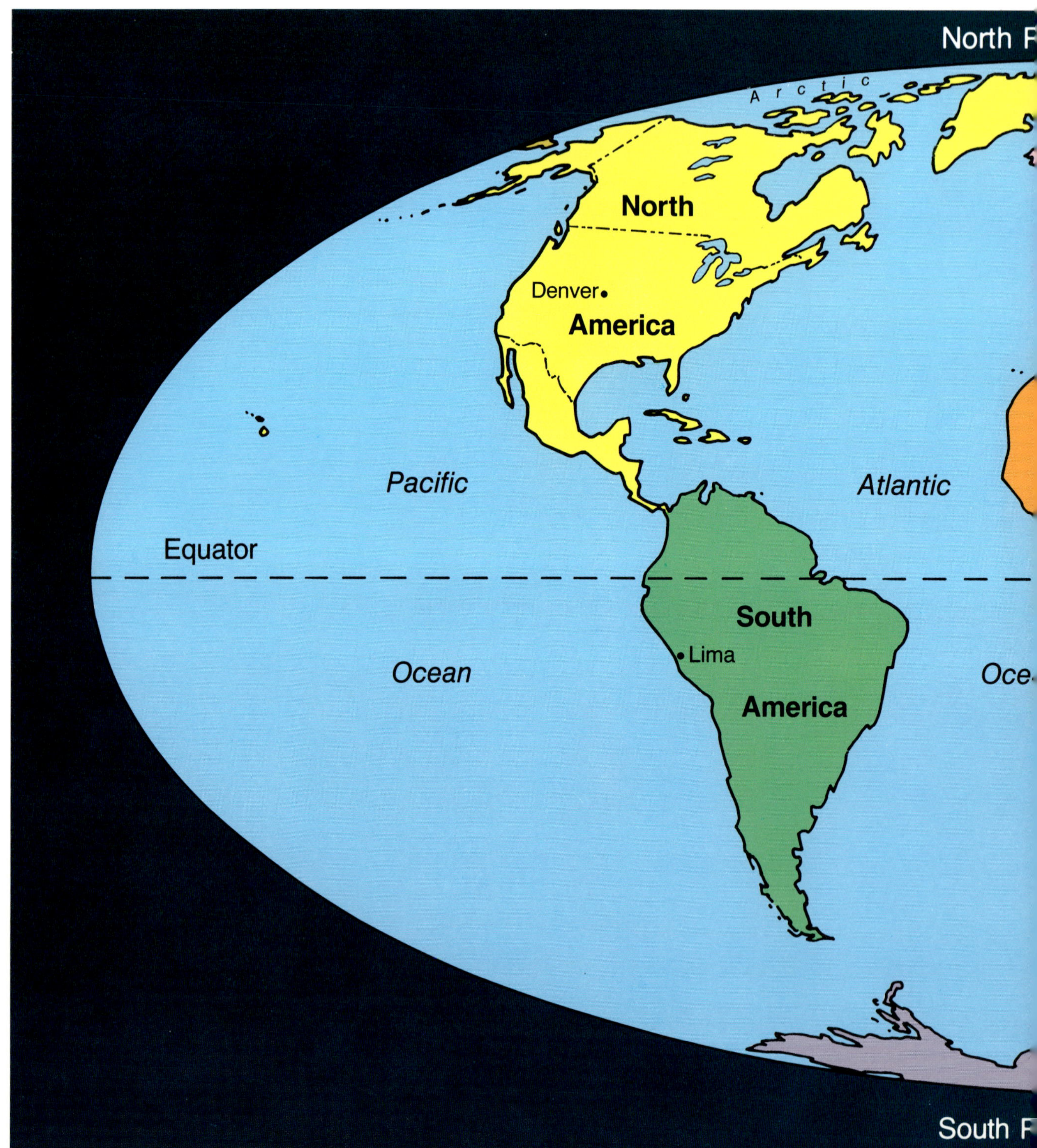

Cities in Other Countries

There are seven continents and four oceans on the earth. On every continent there are cities. This map shows a few of the world's cities.

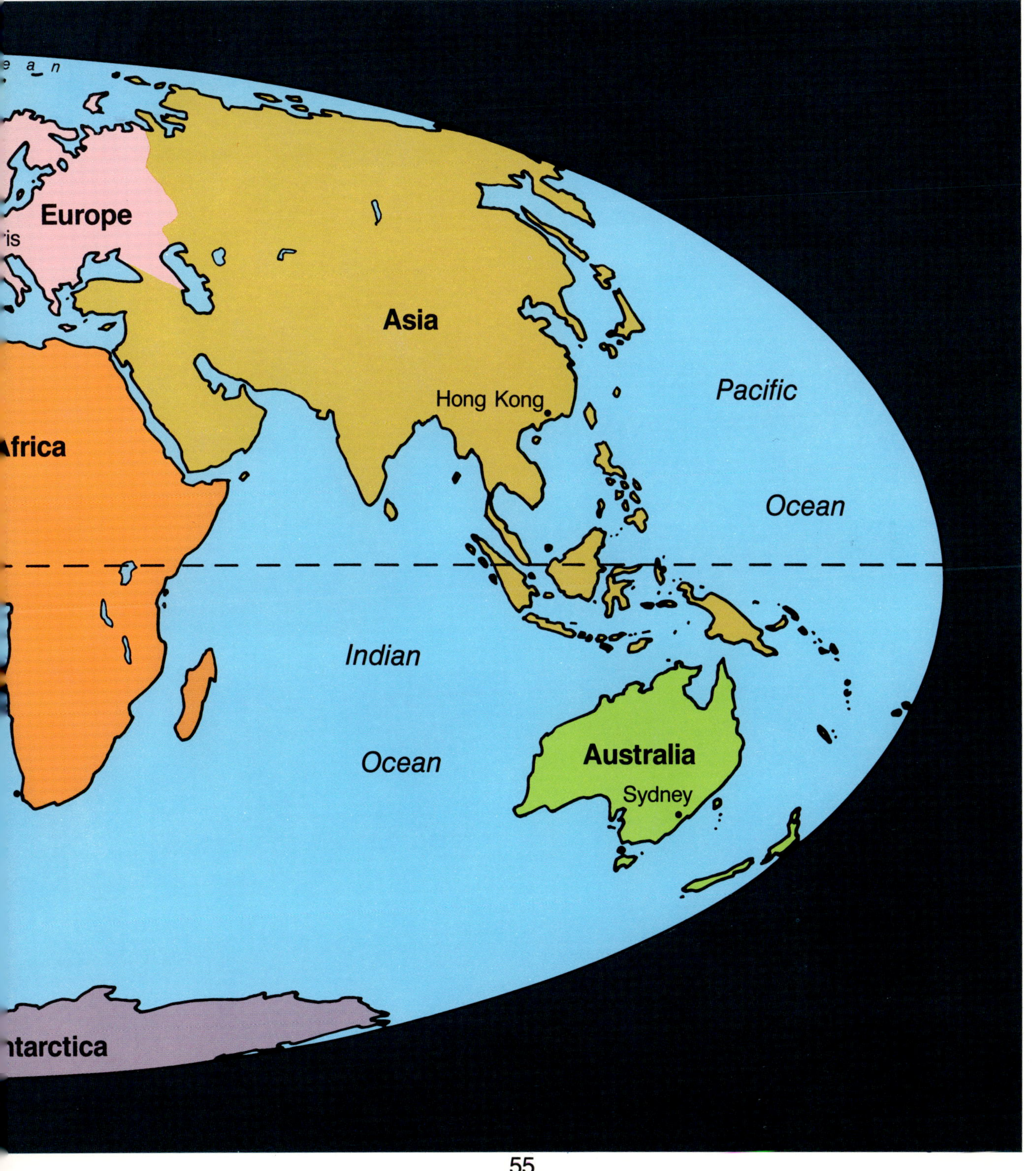

Cities Around the World

These photographs were taken in three of the cities shown on the map of the earth. There are two pictures of each of the three cities. One is an aerial photograph. The other is a ground photograph. The two pictures of each city are not side by side.

Can you match the aerial photographs with the ground photographs of these cities? Look for clues in the photographs that will help you match the pictures.

a

b

c

d

e

f

The three cities shown in the photographs on these two pages are Sydney, Hong Kong, and Denver. What is alike about the cities? What is different? Can you tell which city is which?

There are cities in every part of the world. Think about the people who live in these cities. How do you think they are like the people in your community? How do you think they are different? Would you like to visit people in other cities?